High-Maintenance

High-Maintenance

Stephen Bett

Ekstasis Editions

National Library of Canada Cataloguing in Publication Data

Stephen Bett
    High-maintenance

    Poems.
    ISBN 1-894800-42-7

    I. Title.
PS8553 E834 H53 2004   C811'.54   0301

© 2004 Stephen Bett
Author photo: Erin Bett

Acknowledgements:
The author is very grateful to Langara College for a six month paid leave while he worked on this book.
Poems from this manuscript have appeared in the following: *High Design Refit* (chapbook, Greenboathouse Books, 2002), *Antigonish Review* (Canada), *Aught* (U.S.), *Big Bridge* (U.S.), *BOGG: An Anglo-American Journal*, *Canadian Dimension* (Canada), *Canadian Literature* (Canada), *Eclectica Magazine* (U.S.), *Evergreen Review* (U.S.), *Exquisite Corpse* (U.S.), *Flarestack* (England), *Glossolalia* (Finland), *inter/face* (U.S.), *Ixion* (England), *Jacket* (Australia), *Locust* (U.S.), *Pif Magazine* (U.S.), *Rampike* (Canada), *Real Poetik* (U.S.), *Sepia* (England), *Skanky Possum* (U.S.), *Switched-on Gutenberg* (U.S.), *Tads 5* (Canada), *Terrible Work* (England), *Wascana Review* (Canada), Vancouver Co-op Radio, CFRO.

Published in 2004 by:
Ekstasis Editions Canada Ltd.   Ekstasis Editions
Box 8474, Main Postal Outlet   Box 571
Victoria, B.C. V8W 3S1   Banff, Alberta ToL oCo

THE CANADA COUNCIL | LE CONSEIL DES ARTS
FOR THE ARTS | DU CANADA
SINCE 1957 | DEPUIS 1957

BRITISH
COLUMBIA
ARTS COUNCIL
Supported by the Province of British Columbia

High-Maintenance has been published with the assistance of grants from the Canada Council for the Arts and the British Columbia Arts Board administered by the Cultural Services Branch of British Columbia.

for my sister, Joan, with love and thanks

Contents

News from the Frontal Lobe	9
They Say Bite Me, from the 70th to 20th Parallels	10
Drive, He Said	11
Vapor Trail	12
Only Miracle	13
Socio-Quick Takes	14
One for Massachusetts	15
A Second for Massachusetts	17
One More Go-Round for Mass & Co.	18
Found Poem for the New Hampshire Dead	19
Juliet of the Spirits II: The Future is Millennial	20
Save-On-Black Hole	21
Please Donate This Book	22
Poof, We All Fall Down	23
High-Maintenance	25
High-Maintenance on the Airhead Runway	27
Three Millennial Signs	28
Addendum to 3 Mill: Dr. of the Trench (filed harder & dissed)	31
Gift Rapped	32
Summer Lessons, in the Rainforest	33
Two Ends of the Country, Temporally Speaking	34
News from the Frontal Lobe II (riding vapid transit)	35
Another Knock-Off	36
High Design Refit, after Hollo	37
The Shirts	38
Slow Moving Advice for a 9 Thru 11-Year-Old When He Turns 18	39
Asia: A Grace Note, and Hollow	42
The Big One	44
Usable & Unusable	46
Sonnet on the Aegrotat	48
Quick Exit on the Pharmacy Road	49
Pharmacy Road II (on & off ramps)	50
Dumb Lock, Dumb Luck	52
Stoned Penguin	53

Dehearing the Soaps	54
Mishearing Again	55
To The Mr. Asshole Who Just Stole My Mini-Van	56
Heads Up, Meltdown Coming	57
Head to Head: Roszak Bible to Cosmetics Counter in a Single Generation	59
Head to Head II: Duking it at the Millennium	60
Yachtsperson's Bumper Sticker	62
Prejudice and Pride	63
A Circuitous J'Accuse from a Central Asian Zola	64
Jack Spicer Does Not Know Who He Is (Two Quick Takes)	65
Out in a Blaze of Glory	67
Eleven Out-Takes for a Magazine Editor	68
Cover Story: Soap Culture, Splash 'n Rinse Culture, Petrie Dish Culture—Millennial Drain	70
Snowboarding with Whistler Pornstar	71
Eventual De-Thaw of the Gene Pool	73
News from the Frontal Lobe III (endorsements for the last big three)	75
Nineties Found Poem: A Personal Chronology, with One Year Left to Y2K	76
Hydro Power (Variant: I Know a Woman)	77
Binny & the Jets, 9/11	78
Quick Takes on Mid-Week America I-5, 9/11 and a Half (& counting…)	80
SUV Epiphany at the Upscale Mall	81
Stick-Handling the Times	82
21st c. E– / Voice Mail Excuses for Missing Class	83
Head Games for Prols and the Filthy Rich	85
Radio Clips Dad Missed from the 21st Century (Deflowered, out of the mouths of babes)	87
Psych Nurse	88

News from the Frontal Lobe
(& hold that thought, hard)

Despite what the paranoids, wackos,
& conspiracy nutters believe, the New World Order
isn't really about little pale blue helicopters
crossing prize flatlands in the night
& it isn't about the federales' registration of
aberrant neurotransmitters concealed under
sporting or sub-trade cap logos,
it's about Mono-Culture taking over *my* radio
(& I don't mean their radio or your radio).

Hystereo-talk, trash-talk, psycho-babble, it's all
the same Excited States of Americano to us here in the
chilled out upper terminal states,
when the local eye in the sky air-head breaks in
after the OK Tire ads with "what's your sign," I say
"what's your frequency," & it feels like it's doing
giant copter-blade-wheelies into my head
& its payload wriggles & slithers like the United
Snakes of the World.

Still, there's something comforting about the thought
that while it may be high-tech biochemical bandaids
are holding *my* goddamn brain together,
those wily wingnuts are busy mainlining themselves
direct to the cortex with the steady drip
of synthetic snakeoil.

They Say Bite Me,
from the 70th to 20th Parallels

They're all screaming suing screwing each other
on open mouth radio, head-butting the ref,
drive-by head-bangers (on-board metal bats), road rage
escorts up the driveway
                                      quick update on cinematic
full-tilt in-your-face action picture this—
flavour of the month acid splash on Latino señoritas
no hay de qué, rejected suitors (whose loss of face
riming here one wonders?)
                                          now the latest HDTV
reality dispatch— young video enterprisers offer
pre-wedding pre-scripted choreographed courtship,
instant nostalgia (til el splitto), package B adds
custom sound set-piece love tussle boy tips
girl by Ottawa canal, NYC crews throw on
discreet cameraman nuptial late nite, soft focus
stud/studette wannabes tongue lash, lip-sink splitting
period-theme-wedding mock-cherries

What's it all getting to, where's it all at?
picture-in-picture, *Muthos* R Us the man could
now say, such "jurastic change" my post-literate
college student spells it out, likewise head-butting
himself, on paper, re-vapidized, Spielbergized,
waiting on F/X & financing in place like they say
to make it truly & sincerely yours (& yours)
                                        against all odds
putting the wrap on real-time

Drive, He Said

I'm on The Drive in a, you know,
no-pre-own-challenged CD/bookstore
this VW van parked outside
vintage   decidedly post-hip, styling
retro, psychedelic, block letters
stamped across windshield
                    FUKNGRÜVN

& stencilled on spare tire cover
over front grill

```
            C   L
      U           E
   N                 A
 F                     R
   R                 E
      E           N
            E   O
              Z
```

so we know it's all but psychically disarmed

The twenty-something clerk/proprietor/
                    owner (operator?)
enthusing at me verbatim dialogue
Monkee Mike w/Zappa guesting on
some astrally imploded rerun,

I think, "guys today"
living in somebody *else's* past
Well "hell-o?"… get a life
star turn dude
no problem he says, I'll just
morph into yours

Vapor Trail
for Mark

In 1811 Shelley pronounced the Eucharist
cannibalistic and turned to a half-baked
vegetarian régime and full-flight *doppelgängers*.

Now it's the real late 20th C and when
one says, with filliping smirk,   "Eat Me"
one is not talking even post-millennial
                              transubstantiation

but means while you digest that possibility
your humanoid protein wafer has already
levitated the proverbial coop trailing fin-de-siècle
vapors of aromatherapy and the auto-romance of
strategically pierced body parts.

Only Miracle

Nothing to cheer you, a month's
full spiral of biochemical terror,
know poems won't stand to such miracle

Only miracle in sight, agony will slowly
pool & sheer away, exit, in pieces
you tell me, about the eyes

Now where the poem sits
one wants, desperate, *all* the house
three people close, one view, no
glass screen drawn against them

And when the daily tremors run down
exhausted, tranquilized, forgive me
(repetitious)   I want to dream
my mind flushed

Socio-Quick Takes
(Can Air to Toronto, v. late 20th C)

There are way more white folk   down
town   midtown   right up the Annex   two

thirds seem male   and a whole load of them
for sure   still smoking

One for Massachusetts   (& five serendipities)

There's a poem here somewhere
naked below the dash (you solenoid tease   key
locked in our rental car   •   we're right outside

one *big weathered white clapboard house*
homage chez Olson, 28 Fort Square (2nd fl)
                    Gloucester Harbor

all 94 degrees of it, humid   squinting
sagely tourista, face to Pentax   layered heat
wired skyline to a shrinking
Ten Pound Island   •   the landlord's son-in-law

& I finally abort attempt at auto-break
                    (a guy thing, persistent, our ten-
                    year-old informs his mom
that coat hanger not trusty, rusty enough
abandon handyman to the triple-A pro
w/ the half-ton & winch, plenty
to lift even a virtual Maximus of T

one Big O could find
serendipitous to sing
                    I know a dress just sewed
                                (saw the wind

              blow its cotton
              against her body
              from the ankle
                        so!
              it was Nike

& I too swing manic, intent on relics
local commerce, what's authentic like design-your-own
Nike T's stamped *Cape Ann*

           She
       was going fast
       across the square, the water

       this time of year, that
       scarce

       And the fish

so my wife gunning the rental out front
thinks offal, thinks *visitez les slums*
         Dogtown my
one requisite stop along a stunner coast
coves & ha'bors without end
       the Big Bean
       to Portsmouth & Rye

know I'll dash
off to it also

A Second for Massachusetts

Couple of days off the interstate
we finally manage to unlock
a baffling piece of local
signage

       Boiled Dinner Thursdays

enough to keep one moving, briskly

One More Go-Round for Mass & Co.

Swampscott
Rye Beach
Newfane

Tanglewood
Newport
Lexington

so brief in the loop

Great Scot, why
dammit why, did granny
Macfarlane let them

take her, mere child
out of Fall River MA ?

Yanked some mean spin on the
wheel   w/novel bank shot
right at continental drift

Tampa to Lavoy, Alberta

No sooner fly the great divide
we're a sellout   de-iced,
retrofit in the gene pool

Your hapless mutant emerges
from tweed-curtained swamp

without even a burr

Found Poem for the New Hampshire Dead
for Ginny

"LIVE FREE OR DIE"

Juliet of the Spirits II : The Future is Millennial

Homaging in on Gino Severini's *Le Boulevard*
in the Galleria Nazionale D'Arte Moderna, in the
Villa Borghese, in north-central Roma, the painting
emits a sequence of frenetic flicking sounds

the dark, nouveau sleek woman behind me
fanning herself   (a stylish Latin impatience
with her overloaded program in the
booted up mid-August heat
of tamed Futurist space.

Save-On-Black Hole

> *We are the dust of long dead stars. Or,*
> *if you want to be less romantic, we are*
> *nuclear waste.*
>   Sir Martin Rees, "A Conversation,"
>   *New York Times*, Apr. 28/98

The most unnaturally selected locus in which to procure
Astronomer Royal cousin Sir Martin's new book on
cosmology (intro by S. Hawking) is the promo shelf in front
of the skin & muscle mags adjacent the freeze-dried zone
in the local aluminum-box mega-store
                                        Pretty much akin to
decoding a metonymic universe from the current multiverse
stacked deep in black holes
                            This one's slurping up fluorescent
lite as it slices, dices across the bleary eye
tripping, peaking (as we used to say)
down aisles of diminishing return.

Here you really are like the cyber-manual astronaut
soul-sucked by a "gravitational imprint
frozen in space"
                     You're pasta, astro-babe,
low percentage karma, instant "spaghettification"
layered, 10-D superstring squeezed thru
an "inflationary universe"
                           And near the low-cue checkout,
final buzz of Tim-Oh-Leary time, they'll be pumping in a
second, unplugged Steverino "We are stardust" all the way
from Yasgur's farm to wide-aisle warehouse bulk-world
waiting on options to your choice of slow expanding
flushed out heat-death, or vacuum pull Big Crunch
returning the entire merchandise, as it were,
after its consumption.

Please Donate This Book
(A Reverse Abbie Hoffman)

Smuggle a copy of your last
book through U.S. customs
right on into City Lights
Bookstore
Slip it onto the shelves between
Berrigan & Blackburn

& walk out the door,
for real, as though you'd
planted a silent bomb

thinking it may
or may not go off

in the time it takes to
fly home
to fly down later last chance,
new book under cover of a
real gone world argot

to fly back all your hard copy
pure biodegraded pulp
                          down-

loaded & on your tail
without the lightest trace

POOF, WE ALL FALL DOWN

OK so it's Valentine's Day at work
& those nice people in financial aid have
decorated their reception window with a heart-
felt pair of silhouettes, a fresh young couple
puckering for a frisky little kiss   (nothing
French, nothing leaking, blow dried)   The pony-
tail girl looking pretty much a simp, the boy fore-
head-challenged, like: vacancy, apply within

But it's front page in the dailies & more than an
anchor job on the six o'clock (& the national, &
CNN)   "several complaints" received— *homophobic*
non-inclusive   discriminate…same sex couples
blah blah blah, yada yada yada
                              Administration's
ordered the offending image removed, "consider
the whole community, not just one small [sic, hurl]
group" of the hormonally hard-wired

Then there've been the predictable, helpful
suggestions —bromides— like 10 percent gay smooches
(rimless)   gender-free hands (basted in acid to disguise
skin tone)   except as mere presence might
bring out the suits for thalidomides, &c

Plus we've had the expected wimp-outs from the
Politically Cowed   'they could, like…anyways, both
be guys or girls'   —even extreme bovine   'they
could, like…you know, both be dudes or babes'
When what it undoubtedly comes down to, of course,
& the issue is truly international & applies, name
just one, to the Kappa logo stitched all over
Juventus of Turin
                           —the real rub everyone's overlooked,
an advancing case of "ageism" afflicting the cerebro-
genitally challenged (formerly, dickheads)   Material
boys & girls, this other balkanized frame of a
GLOBAL* fashion file.

* "Gay Lesbians and/or Bisexuals at L……"

High-Maintenance

Walk in the park, day bright and fair,
Flip a cripple a nickel,
Kick a pigeon in the air.
                                    Paul Violi

The latest directives apropos *Appropriate Terminology
Regarding Persons With Disabilities* have now been handed
down to the oft dissed elites on the front lines, and they
don't come cap in hand

                      All system-wide resources (human
and pro-rata) are instructed in the following approved
usage—

- "Person with a developmental disability" is prescribed over "retarded," retard, moron, etc.
- "Person with cerebral palsy," instead of "spastic," spas, gimp/gimper
- ditto "with a mental illness, or person who has (eg. schizophrenia)," rather than "mentally ill," fruit-bar, wacko, fuck-up/fuck-head
- "Person resident in trailer park milieu," in place of low rent, t-p trash, loser, &c.

                         A further, State
requirement (Ministry *Guidelines for Inclusive Curriculum*) cautions
each vehicle of delivery to ask itself "Have I avoided ablist, sexist,
racist, and classist humour and other forms of ablism, sexism,
racism and classism" (incl. N.Y. School "Personism")⸮

                                                        And a final,
standing 'reminder' comes direct from the "disability advocacy
community," advising those non-challenged present imperfect flukes
they push, and pull, their luck as "TABs" —ie. the (quote, underlined)
temporarily able-bodied (end quote)

                                        Esp. now they've 'sourced'
a protocol, are this point in time 'impacting' it all over the trenches
and will be 'accessing' the synapses of response   —now is the time for
all "differently abled" persons to come to the aid of the pluperfect, re-
program the techno-serfs "high-maintenance"
                                        high flyers, lone flyer
                                        top run and gun

surfing colourless, bloodless sites
for a target lock-on

High-Maintenance on the Airhead Runway

So like we now know it's okay after all
the show can go on, & on, in clean cut Atlantic City
Miss America 1999 has been crowned while *wearing
an insulin pump…only the second woman with a
disability* (reports Reuters) to head off
in such rarefied air

Which goes to show that in the high roller world of the
indoor runway, the notion "handicap" can count for
as little below as above a plunging neckline
And that high-maintenance, at this
singularly developed stage,
means there're more than a handful of sweet slots
in which to feed synthetic, engineered or implanted
substances in the low percent shot to payoff
that is even loosely aesthetic, pancreatic
& cerebral

Three Millennial Signs

      1.

Then there was the one about the two otherwise
delightful, hearing-impaired college students
exempted from the required English course
on the grounds their writing skills are not up
to scratch, literally, & therefore should
not be subjected to the subtleties
of detection
              Instead they've been accessed,
thru Counseling, into a three-credit course in
Oral Communication, each with her own fully-
funded interpreter all signed up &
ready to download the nuanced
niceties of effective
extemporaneous
delivery

2.

Then there was the one about the suspected
psychopath (w/a history) who in a moment of
irritating self-doubt put his fist through the
classroom wall, handed in a neatly ambiguous
death threat to his teacher, & followed her
home every day for three weeks   His lawyer
had him reinstated on campus (legal bills
siphoned out of operating funds) after a 48-
hour expulsion & a promise to recontinue
medication
                College counsel perfected the double
Bail, recommended accelerated graduation
& shut down the fisti-guy's files
(under provisions in FOIPOP*)
                              Our whacked out
wacko then shuffled off to sign-on across town
as a "special needs" aide in a downscale primary
school portable, setting it on auto-implode
before he could ever run out of Charter**
buttons worth his past or future
to keep on selectively poking

---

*   "Freedom of Information and Protection of Privacy" legislation
** Constitutional "Charter of Rights and Freedoms"

3.

Then there was the one about the student who
adamantly insisted his teacher never allow mention
of the word "Nike" in their poetry seminar–
under advisement he might be "suiciding"
himself, pronto please
Something about cults & comets   People
cinder-tracked where only space is deep,
37 of them, signed out
                            74 cast-off
group-discount, terminally clipped
grounded & de-swooshed
Air Jordans

Addendum to 3 Mill : Dr. of the Trench
(filed harder & dissed)

Then there was the 18-year-old
boffo freshman who, queried by his long-
swerving "course deliverer" from higher.edu
(tho herself only waist-high to hallway
vending machine) why he's already missed
three weeks by mid-term,
allows as "your class just isn't
working for me"

to which she's maybe supposed to go
like yeah, what-ever, or upchuck
some serious GPA-proof coin.

GIFT RAPPED

It's now politically untoward to refer
to one's intellectual orientation, that's elitist,
even street smarts is leaking some of its hot air
to nu-age footwear   We're not allowed to mention
"gifted" kids, and of course no-one nowadays is
literally a dumb fuck, just an unloaded piece
in a double-blind test-site sponsored by
Attitude +

And likewise for sure it's always been
cool to blab down, post-game, yawn,
you know, in cable-sports monotone
everyone knows words is for
the anal, priss, candy ass (what-ever

Then there's Post-Sec Education polls, decades
worth, break numbers right down the middle
(& that's *within* the household
                                       First row
says school tax should "transition" the
neighbor's little boom-box rapper
into techno-peasant training
                                      Second,
that cross-street mill rates "credentialize"
our own kids straight into made-for-TV
medicine or law, & don't forget to
dummy down the bar for maximum
post-polling, pre-election
bounce

Summer Lessons, in the Rainforest

Even on holiday, surrounded by west coast rainforest,
we can't escape the latest in skill-testing bi-cultural
awareness
                For sensitivity to the non-inclusive interests
of local tree-hugger and aboriginal spiritualist
our tourist pamphlet offers the totemic import
of "culturally modified trees"
                              while to alert us to anti-
social practices in the semi-wild, the radio news warns
of a 59-year-old apprehended for pleasuring himself
against a cemetery tombstone— "offering indignities
to a monument marking human remains"
                                        The lesson here,
apart from a kind of old- and mid-growth lushness
of euphemism, appears to indicate that cultural
adaptation can be as simple as handing a few well-
placed whacks, on tree or stump, as a preferred way
to ward off, or repulse, all manner of evil spirit
whether emanating from sky or from under ground.

Two Ends of the Country, Temporally Speaking

One:

They want us to understand that, while discomforting,
clitoral mutilation, culturally sanctioned wife abuse, daughter-
in-law dowry murder— all continue to blend the 'mosaic'
that is the country's future.
At least, it's a rare case of tripartisan cooperation.   And thus
very Parliamentarian.   (Badges, stickers all around.)
Right. Center. Left.   Cheap labour, discount party member-
ships, budget-priced heartthrob, post-bled— not to mention
certain monthly dues.

And the slash (dot) net reduction?   The "multi"
in multicult.   80% draw
on a 20% source.

Two:

We say you *know* it's the '90s when the local band chief
leaves his Saab running to head in for his morning
Starbucks.
In the semiotic puffs of exhaust one can still read the desk clerk
at the native-run lodge actually venting (after a German bus tour
clears out of the lobby) about those "friggin' Clayoquot tree-
huggers" gambling away all future enterprise with offshore
casino consortiums.

News from the Frontal Lobe II (riding vapid transit)

We live in a time when mindlessness has become
a profession replacing the mere state it used to be.
                             Ed Dorn

As fin de millennium enters New World Monoculture
the proverbial question of sizing the gap between
generations   (presently @ and un-@)
is becoming increasingly moot   We're simply
down to the stickier points of symbiosis   Of who's
'downloading' versus who's 'logging on'

And it doesn't only merge online, vapid transit,
E-Zee one-stop "thought shrinkage," eyeball surfing
the latest "shockventures"—
                             one palpable, if lo-tech,
version is hotline radio, open mouth segued into
mouth breather   The gulp of transmission that
registers multiple time zones   At precisely which point
cue breathless promo for up and coming
'docu-citement':
                Don't miss the Superstar of Serial
Killers live right here on Network blah blah..

So no problem, some syndicated wag
talks the talk "tyranny of trash"
"decade of dross"   But we still site
preference for less alliterative, more
progressive terms
                        Like
cycling loose testosterone
score half as (dot) net
loss / losing / losers

Another Knock-Off

the language, the language!
             WCW

This is just to say
I have tasted
all your knock-
offs

Koch
Dorn (both)
Dudek
Norris
Berkson (w/ Fagin & Padgett)
and Webb

and which
you left lying
around
under wraps

Forgive me
they still
knock me out
what poems
you found
in that open
icebox

High Design Refit, after Hollo

on the high designer bar,
when we tip
the barista
we say, "no problema,
barista"

THE SHIRTS
for Pam & Nolan

You ask me what I'd
wear each Friday
& I know if two are long shots,
relegation zone, they're all cross-
town traffic, like the man said   Derby,
which includes
                  Tottenham
                  Everton
                  Lazio (two)

        even up for Hearts
if the money's there, & half
Scots yourself   (to my quarter
How could anyone root round
a Man U spice-throb
a grass stained Butt ?

Surer bet to ask your eleven-
year-old   so blithely, blondly
handsome, dressed
at least for
                  Arsenal
                  Newcastle
                  Borussia Dortmund

like it's never too far, he thinks,
get down, boogie   max out those bands
of colour—insignia—logo   the way they
rapid fire the retina, trans-

continental, your move

Slow Moving Advice for a 9 Thru 11-Year-Old When He Turns 18

Don't forget the clean
gaunch ethos, little guy,
works like a charm, each citizen

preclude all manner emerg.,
trauma, late-date surprise
any list you incline to think of

May be only way to wear double
community standards   Take care of
business both ends, as they say

lookin' good best of times, well
hosed in worst, this so you bath
shower, change it up—   daily

pretty set, even for life,
blank out on all but your own
inestimable comfort

It's like you said a year
ago "it's like when you're
born your brain washes out,

maybe it's so there's enough
room in there for your life"

So you can add to store-
house chip *tabula rasa*—
clean gaunch, cleaned brain

more likely pair than your
père boy guilted up with
Mens sana in corpore sano

Greek, Latin, head boy caning
'privileges'   Forever Descartes
to your "Exist. precedes ess."

& natural too to retrieval age
parked before the keyboard
squirm to shift out of a cheap

wedgie, likewise gene pool
mea gloria fides indeed,
biz for the family biz

Even the uncontested you'll
want no distraction, irritant,
you know a wedge'd

take the eye off any move
to bend a corner, return a
slam in kind—   at source

best bet yet, detour traps
means no wedge at all, non-band-
roll, pure 100% brushed cotton

hanging in there with style

ASIA: A GRACE NOTE, AND HOLLOW

All evening you've wept
discreetly   intermittent
days hinged by a rueful
disavowal   You'd held

the sweet little thing like a broken
mirror   two pair of eyes
freeze-locked   other organs
wasted   It even eases

one straight arrow squeeze thru
abdominal wall   slips into
herself
         only a woman could
mean "graceful"

Or this difference from early days
the kids just a few quick
bursts   lack faith some
pale future the real
throat-grabber

Or that when it does get there
our eldest surprises from
behind   her shoulder-jab outside
to stare it down   bite heads
off stupid flowering
bromides

        our youngest
instantly disarmed   beads
across your neck

Taking turns I model
detached   one slight damp
eye
      I'm *always* slow
it rings back hollow

enough to refill some
kind of further   less
suspected
        more suspect
loss

The Big One (a/counting lesson)

Been around the block
serious hedging   shuffler

needs work, ditto—

fear & loathing, income,
seratonin levels

Most of it *is* crap
like they say, each one
a discernment

Count them backwards
then, one hand, no clapping

no recourse resource remorse
to do, make, turn it

more than half over   —zero
force hand any over

Leaves barely a finger hang-

ing onto those one truly
cares for, wife, children

And the others sitting
there, holding only doubt

stupendously under
played

Usable & Unusable Terms

> *We, too, may turn diseases into pearls.*
> Coleridge

Try to hit it head on
each term a revolving door,
glassed in, slivered gaps

flag it—   mood swing, disorder,
breakdown, X or Y-attack, & always
the ubiquitous *classic, clinical*

The French, suitably uncanny, get
closest   *la maladie du doute*
nail this translucent surround
                    if not its
chronic little terrors

When it peaks one thinks,
almost musically, "any day now"
not *release* exactly, Dylan's,
or that reedy heart shattering
falsetto at Big Pink

one reaches, instead, for the post-
modern, the pharmaceutical,
coinage of the pro-active

Like they spell *relief* in the ads
so slow you can only gut it thru,
headache or gas

gassing oneself
in the head ?

Finally, a question of one's
choice of exit

same way even Microsoft will
filter such distinctions,
more a romanticism than that
nation of "speeding" rationalists—

you are advised simply to
click twice either on "suspend"
or "shut down"

Sonnet on the Aegrotat
for Roger

It can be a costly mistake to float numbers on any-
thing loosely billed as "the Finals," gambling your one
shot option on extreme fulfillment could ride out the
hyperplot that is new expanded, wireless mother earth,

even the most myopic bureaucracies & ministries can
see third party payback in the user friendly approach,
rolling out the aegrotat carpet on seemingly sedate, if
distant, compassionate grounds   Think of it as

hitching airborne on your late, great *average*   Think
of them working you out as secured funding, your
flight path never more than en route & infinitely *mean*
about going down where all runways are virtual, all

ground shuttles fictive undeployable, like sonnets
spread thin over time lacking landing gear

Quick Exit on the Pharmacy Road

So what the hey it's really
looking up all right
one can weigh in
mid-evening

dose it up double, whatever,
pale orange, techno-pact
easy, conveniently scored

Knock out horse
ten ton truck, turn

down headlight
full reverse-astral,
return sender

Start slow-mo' like numbness
like blacktopping cracks
each fibre, filament

then drive straight
out of one's mind
—at speed

Pharmacy Road II (on & off ramps)

      1.

Formerly known as
"dropping some…"
               or better
"do" a couple lines
(straight off the razor

Rock a few brain cells
blow off like quick
dispatches
Hyperventilate

Roll five-dollar bills

2.

Now we're a seismic
upgrade   —certified
License to chill
twice daily

One ninety-five a month
(sans dispensary

Want the edge off the rock,
quake scaled down
                The numbers
one would simply think
more passable

Dumb Lock, Dumb Luck

Brain lock, doctor doctor says
stick shift stuck in
caudate nucleus   (Ouch)
Can't even run an
effin' red light when
one needs to (don't
try this at home)

One did feel sat upon
in the midst of it
Flood engine
Wait only to get
blindsided

Then truly invaded, sirens
          (your ears only)
adrenal revved to upper
register   (Screech
one said)
And not til way later
joke up a patent for
serious slimming

Which one could also,
macabre, even
Byronesque
ride up & down scales
literally, his own
dumb luck
Especially après bingeing

Not a chance at starving
out all that bloodied
incoming traffic

Stoned Penguin

Well, I'll be
jiggered & jaggered
& jaromir jagred

Dehearing the Soaps

She loved him so much
his tail bone disconnected.

Mishearing Again

Put your pillows
all in a line
I hear Madonna on my
daughter's ghetto-blaster

good advice far as I
can tell, & serviceable
dense in possibility

Beaten to submission, fluff,
shoot in a row (quack quack)
prioritize pleasure partners, less
extreme than barrel sports

advance posture, soft
linkage stuffed boy toys,
dispensing S & M instruction

Most of it, second thought,
woman with a case of
been there, done that
the fame vehicle thing

just stacks up mileage
til another choice of
waxing

To The Mr. Asshole
Who Just Stole My Mini-Van

While you're busy B & E-ing your way through
South Surrey don't think of yourself
as some kind of outlaw rebel you're just
a scummier than usual entrepreneurial sideshow

And as for So. Surrey it just might be a case
of heading home to hit up the neighbours
a matter of moving product, like they say,
market invasion, delayering the middle row
demerging the back row, retail the niche, out-
sourced driver, maximize fits-all, downscale
back-loaded, nonvalue-added

Then they all go option playback, their 15 of fame,
validates the big ticket make mine payback
second place is first loser, suppose they
nail the dickhead (major if) luck out on
road rage, maybe road kill
                          surprise— balaclava
stalker, serial pervert, parole psycho, you just know
media scrum will smarm the asshole right
down the halls of plea bargain a most
courtly "Mister."

Heads Up, Meltdown Coming

Our all-time favorite title, shrink-wrapped, behind
the counter, local corner store— the altogether prepossessing
Young and Wet

And now twenty years later Monica & Bill, respectively,
nine muse-worthy blow jobs that shook the media, as well as
tighten up the beltway, tune up the Bible Belt
In his Grand Jury testimony Slick Willie "deplores" his
persecutors' "illegal leaking" of, among other things,
the famous blue DNA-stained dress

But the people are more savvy than the nerdy Mr. Starr
(no swingin' Ringo in his quasar chamber)— lying about sex
as ancient as Hollywood, young as its mythed-up pilgrims

The Networks breathlessly worry that "viewers are on
disconnect" about Oval sex —despite CNN's efforts
(eminently successful) to keep ratings up with 25 hour days
on in-coming third party fellatio, Helms-Burton cigars,
did she go down just for a job, &c.

while the over-extended economies of Thailand Indonesia
Japan Russia Brazil are facing "meltdown," son of
alzheimer Ronnie's "trickle-down"

Meantime the only other media fix this summer/fall is
the homer race, leaving a barely noticeable few of us to ask
the obvious question: why don't they just the hell leave
steroid-free Roger Maris alone

except as that would be a matter of too much for the purists, not enough for the lo-lust neo-puritans of body-sculpted McPopulist morality*

* Mark McGwire's probably a real nice guy—and certainly pretty charitable for an 8 mil. per annum, undoubtedly back-loaded ballplayer—but the one thing he *does* trail in common with the Jerry Falwells of the day is the lingering sense that the size of the spin is really greater than the flight.

Head to Head: Roszak Bible to Cosmetics Counter in a Single Generation

The caption under the 'community' tab slash marketing
organ's fashion-spread photo showing one lip-enhanced dept
store "Vendor" layering what looks like half a tube of gel gloss
over the sacrament-receptive mouth of a second, coiffed,
flash tranced consumer reads   *Counter Culture*

proving, if you've managed to hang with this planet thru its
latest warp-speed time curve, what goes round comes round
up to & including even the argot du jour
                                              wherein one ex-"head's"
heavy-duty socio-fashion code is a current airhead's
lip-job, fattening out the full 180

like from the making of a Theodore Roszak to the makeover
of clerical counter as meta-altar, a kind of total worship-
ready @ Gen. Bible Lite
                          And you know that's a case of internal
threat on mode 'de-target' & 're-track'   —counting product update

that'll make your head spin inside mirror & chrome, your
olfactories bend days-ya-view to rites for mouth breathers,
your lips move within the mold that feeds them strategic
outcomes from known revisionist sources.

Head to Head II: Duking it at the Millennium

The caption beside the 'community' tab slash marketing organ's front page photo-spread announces a *Ruckus* Four snappy freeze-frame photos narrating a local street-corner duke out   Twenty-something guy, stocky, lank dark hair, swarthy, high cheek bones, beady eyes, worn two-tone football jacket pushing a giant M (Michigan?)

jeans, mtn boots, peeling around from the driver's side, car dead-stopped in intersection, to accost a pedestrian he's evidently "bumped" on cross walk and who's just hammered his fist along our driver's Main Machine

Second and third photos show "pedestrian," a full head taller, older (late 50s?), looking v. much the grumpy / sour-face / mean-mouth disciplinarian-type football coach   Flings the dude guy, shoulder first, onto the trunk of his surprisingly nondescript, white, four-door sedan, cuffs him on the forehead

The last picture shows the now macho-compromised "motorist" caught, head still a-swivel, somewhere between offense and defense   Sidelong corner-eye contact, finger pointing obtusely at "coach," driver's legs stiffly apart, back on heels, splay-foot

It all reads like a magic marker play, four parter,
under gridiron colours two looming background
signs— red/white one flags photographer's own
low-brow rag behind red/blue Sally Ann,
likewise full block coverage, even odd
ideologues, for our info-tainment

Plus one does notice, creditably, the closing shot
black and white —a sequence played to the socio-
sporting annals   Two "combatants" like split-
ends left out at the millennial
line of scrimmage

Yachtsperson's Bumper Sticker

If it's blowing

I'm coming

Prejudice and Pride (found poem)

"We were hoping to ball
you at the sea."

A Circuitous J'Accuse from a Central Asian Zola

Chingiz Aitmatov, the gifted Kirghiz novelist and
member of the Supreme Soviet (tho hardly a rogue apologist),
has the shell-shocked hero of his 1980 naturalist novel
restored to health, if not full ideology, in the laboratory
of manual labour on the chilling steppes of Kazakhstan.
Put most roundly, "the empty Sarozek desert gave two gifts
…its air, and camels' milk. *The air was virgin clean*"
the milk, one assumes, drawn likewise—
practically irradiated.

But stay with it. More recently the experiment must be
re-cast. Much elapsed flashing of light. We find, same
glassy glow of time and place, and a mere 15–30 k from
several villages, the Soviets had had a 20 year blast
400+ above-ground tests, check out 26 hundred
Hiroshimas.   Soldiers ordered peasants out of doors so
they and their livestock could be unaffectedly monitored.
Herds of sheep shake, rattle and keel, their coats
appear to sizzle with the rush in atmospherics,
heat wavy silhouettes, slow-mo' mushroom cloud.

Now decades from their first live-air shower, villagers
turn up facially deformed. Head to heel in lesions.
The g.p. of all re•poo•blics still up-wind behind
their out-of-step author.   A central Asian Zola, he pains-
takingly rolls each die across his work-table—
proud ethnic Yedigei, his renowned camel, "the great
wide spaces—Sary-Ozeki," undulating Aral', and
much for granted one's instinctual resources
for a brute mass survival.

Jack Spicer Does Not Know Who He Is
(Two Quick Takes)

> *Rabbits do not know what they are.*
> Jack Spicer

    1.

Contrary to ontological and empirical evidence
a Jack Spicer, recently referred to at my aunt's
funeral, is putt-putting away in boorjaw central
the interior playland   —three full decades
after his death.

The usual suspect links are duality, polarity
a spicey poesy *at the gates of existence…*
in Kelowna.
        For further *folding*
of the intelligence of
the composition of
the real.

New Critical transceiver mechanisms
pickt up *something*
from the outside
coming in.
        (The "duh" factor.)
Blazing messages out of
the rough. *Dictation* on the roll.
Lay it up short. Low-flyer
low-ghost (-spin

down to two eminences grises
and a single divan   the final
word on pin placement
a remaking of the real
is at stake.

2.

Not even creepy-crawling in rush hour
semi-alert to some 20-something on-the-
make novelist pumped 'n ready to splash
w/ his one-wad a.m. theory (on Gzowski
      or Gabereau—
a numinous linkage between baseball
and the tarot

it's the guy's fey persistence keeps jarring
the wheel, I vent air (stopped for a light) at the
stone deaf radio, "Jack Spicer whizzed that
one out of the park 35 years ago"
and probably didn't really mean to

anyway he couldn't have been that un-
calculated in practice of his own sole
life and outside rimes
and mimes.

Out in a Blaze of Glory

The Figure of Inward
checked in with "the real,"
a thing "tensed"
"imaged"
   I wanted here to argue,
he said, I wish to place here
to fold one with the other, like
(he's spiced up *en robe*) the "terrible"
the "profound"

But o gawd, he drawled,
jutted, flat out (Dudley
Do-Right my wife called him)
my teeth in the mirror green
this morning—outrageous that
gooey line of night
deposit
    Jacked up
Rich in the affairs of his
out-shocked
estate

Which was, true to its
promise, a real seasoned
act to follow
to follow

Eleven Out-Takes for a Magazine Editor

> *Your poems are a <u>hoot</u>—very nasty, very caustic, and yet, oddly loving. I suspect you have as much fondness for your targets as you do contempt….your work is most intriguing…*

Right, love ya'
All the way up the intrigue

       *

Hoot Hoot
Love those Hooters

       *

Rootin' tootin'
Your lingo's suspect,
suspect

       *

Hooters?   Fondlers?
Suspect   Target

       *

Tough love
Odd love   Don't
love yr odds,
love

       *

Beans, beans
the musical fruit,
the more they bite
the more you toot

        *

Tout de suite
Zoot suit

        *

Target fondness
Bull's eye
Bull's breath?
Bite me

        *

Bin shootin' any?
Hootenanny?

Make it moot?

        *

Retro   Suck
Like Mister Wieners say,
"you puke-suck"

        *

Real hoot y'self
Hoot, hoot

Road-kill

Cover Story: Soap Culture, Splash 'n Rinse Culture, Petrie Dish Culture—Millennial Drain

VANESSA TO MAURICE:
"Take Your Lips Off Of Hannah!"

Take Off Your Lips Of Hannah ?
Lips Of Your Hannah Take Off ?

Lips.   Hannah.   Take off,
eh ?
           Off of.

Just the lips.
Cultured.

Snowboarding with Whistler Pornstar

In the inevitable upscale boarder shops one can
barely move for rows of designer merchandise &
collectibles   T-shirts tuques stickers the u-
biquitous fat-edge time-pieces (timed pieces?)
Each with a pesky little message to impart

The Pornstar brand seems to have the head run on
market share, with its timely jump to post-
season casuals   Still room to book ahead
you get
               CAMP PORNSTAR
           We put the log to the beaver

Followed by aural error morphs into oracular eros
Trans-cultural gender graphics fronting messages like

BEN DOVER
               DIVER DOWN
                              JUST A-HEAD

Even the well turned
               I'D RATHER BE DRIVING
               A VULVA

While for the wishful thinker cum self-starter
there's the requisite ball cap fielding outer
& inner wear   Like (tellingly) attracts like
Peaked & lettered headgear reading
                              Pussy Magnet

One is simply assumed
to get on down & take one's
pick

Eventual De-Thaw of the Gene Pool

Back on the old stomping grounds
as they used to say   pre neuro-freako
this half-thrashed little quarter-ton
parked smack in front

                         flip ancient postcards   pickup
                         the main drag   friday nite
                         we *really* say 'let's go check
                         stock'??

Couple useful bumper stickers
on board   full kudos civic
growth 'n duh'velopment

Mounted one side of chrome work
our little trucker advises

                 ORGASM DONOR

the other pissing pithily

                 SAVE THE PLANET
                    kill yourself

Resonant practicalities   (we all *polis*-eyed)
micro/macro for sure   every mucho
out there

                        à la lingo of les
                        locals fasts food—

                                             Hot Eats
                                             Cool Treats

Or rather menus downright budget-rite
cold storage   low-cost eco-terror eyes

Lookin' but a touch iffy on who or
what auto-stall love-stutter
                              squeezed
aboard airtight bag

recycles post-haunts
                    (ditto asphyxia
return flight traffic
shufflin' off
DOA'd

News from the Frontal Lobe III
(endorsements for the last big three)

In the '80s God was a pretty successful fund-
raiser, marketeer, Praise the Lord Pass the Loot.
Until the little cable heart throbbers got caught
stuffing their polyesters (& their off-air boxers).
Kicking back the juice.
                         Now the Big One's
been inked for the millennial Zeitgeist— as a
Fashion Accessory.   Right out there with the Rottweiler
& the half-aspirated tongue shtud.

Exhibit uno grosso, predictably, is tattoo obligato
on the pin-up bopper du jour—extreme navel—
shaking his mojo on MuchMusic.   Signs on as "my heart
is totally into Jesus."   Which after a K-12 diet
of "feel good" & "self-advocate" (intermediate thru
accelerated) essentially means "up yours I'm special
go stencil in your own deep skin statement."

Still, notwithstanding the quick draw of a hot surface,
even our accessorized Main Mutha' has a couple
rivals on the billboard that's today's leasable body-part—
designer head lobes laser-etched in digital "cha-ching" &
share-splitting "swoosh."   Or we should just call it
(& pourquoi non?) a corrective tick, or tic?   Certain affirmations.
Well as ghost sighting.   Like some 'flash' trinity
from a decidedly 'happening'
Endorsement World.

Nineties Found Poem: A Personal Chronology, with One Year Left to Y2K

1.

sweaters (cotton; acrylic)
cowboy boots (Boulet)
headbands (Fila)
toiletries (Colgate; Mitchum)
new age (Tangerine Dream; P. Buffett)
sport socks (LeVI'S)
vests (leather; suede)
tanks (budget; travel)
ear plugs (silicone)
boxers (various)
YJ/TJ (Hunter green)
central/eastern Euro-fiction (inter-/post-bellum)
T's (Premier; Serie A)
Hotspur (FA; reserves)
malamute (Alaskan)

2.

icebags (wraparound)
innerwear (Zoloft/Effexor/Rivotril, extra strength)
Netscape (E-zines; Fanzines)

Hydro Power (Variant: I Know a Woman)

Hot damn I love it, her
sarcasm oozes just so
it leaves a puddle on the

kitchen floor   What can I
say what can I do
my mouth waters even

there, backed up, all over
myself —indeterminate present
She could show still

hydrate the dryness that
surrounds us, & why not
generate a little new static

across the line (old, old
vibrations, as they say)
Equally, I think, was 'lookin

good', & even then on-line
forever, it looks like,
taking aim

BINNY & THE JETS, 9/11

Okay, so how about branch London
World Trade Centre II   Tie in nice with the quainter
sporting shrines, Craven Cottage or the Vicarage Road
Star-stud'd ownership just might fancy a bit of local
flambée steel, takeovers on the up & up
as they say, up to your 'double'
world-class implode

But we're all hip to these encore CNN plots—
running split-screen, agit-*pop*, bumper-strip
narratives   It's exclusive Global Village
cross-ref'd like those movie star charts
                    (it's the linkage, stupid)
calculated to "Six Degrees of Separation"

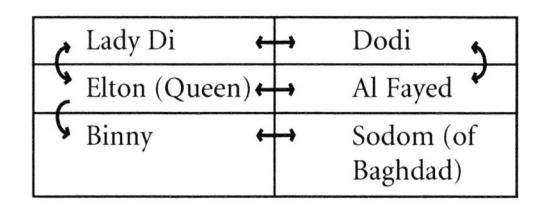

Lady Di ↔	Dodi
Elton (Queen) ↔	Al Fayed
Binny ↔	Sodom (of Baghdad)

         *   *   *

Last season's drive-thru journalism cast flowers
piled higher at proverbial palace gates
the Day Lady Di'd   But this fall pilot
                 "Ground Zero"
more handy little flags, first run info-

mournings segued thru Designer News
'airing' how-to briefs on milling
spores down-home (y'all) in
kitchen, basement

Pushing the 'envelope,' we'd call it,
without risk of breathing in
                              A definite
capital 'R' Ratings spike for sure,
all but back up
the satellite

Quick Takes on Mid-Week America I-5, 9/11 and a Half (& counting…)

Every third or fourth car
with "the flag" glued on a
window like barred optics

and two nifty bumper stickers
riding counter-point:

> I FOUND JESUS
> He was behind the couch
> all along

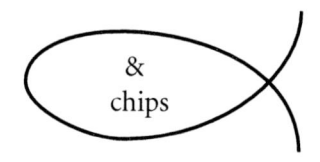

&
chips

Still waiting, though, for that
illusive "dream ticket"—
Fundependent Party '04

Osama & Falwell,
the Bin & Jerry Show

SUV Epiphany at the Upscale Mall

Smartly apropos Whalen's *If You're So
Smart, Why Ain't You Rich?*
it's perennial empty returns, til this year's
bumper crop   Of which,
eminently serviceable
                        And fully loaded

Couple high-enders   Breezy riders
Cruisin' the lot, lookin' somewhere to dock,
thought bubble thinks *rendezvous?*
—outing one's personalized plates

First en parade, as they say,
the incorrigible dame "JEEPSY"
And riding her hatch the low-
flying wedge "MR BENZ"   (oh yeah)
—uppity leasee, spunked on
by the tailgate cadet
Cool in her slip-stream
dumping future options,
along with plenty blanks

Stick-Handling the Times

Used to be a case of
"coming on to,"
decline the skinny on
all sorts of gelled
possibility

Now it's "hitting on,"
which evidently
prefers to conjugate
the deep bruise
over the sticky
flick

21ST C. E– / VOICE MAIL EXCUSES FOR MISSING CLASS

I won't be making it to class today due to lack of gas in my car. My mother omitted to leave me money to fill up the car.

*

I have to miss your [1:30] class to pay some bills. Like my Master Card bill? And the bank closes at like 5:30?

*

I'm going to be sick tomorrow. And maybe a couple of days after, OK?

*

Since this is UBC's reading break, I can't go [come] to classes because I used to study at UBC [flunked out] and my parents don't know I am studying at this college now [flunk*ing* out] . I don't dare to tell them that because I don't know what would happen to me [tuition fees here being half price / half in my pocket 'n all] .

*

I don't do Wednesdays.

*

This is the only week during term when I could get a discount rate to Mazatlán / Cancún / Puerto Vallarta.

*

I am quiet sorry for missing class but, as of Friday I had my tongue pierced. It makes it quiet hard to talk and it hurts quiet badly....I hope there isn't any problems.

*

I have to miss class next week because I'm a bridesmaid at my girl-friend's bikini beach [starter-] wedding— isn't that like soo cool?!— in Mazatlán / Cancún / Puerto Vallarta.

*

I'm sorry I had to miss the last three weeks of classes. My family is Greek so my Dad locked me in my room due to finding there were boys at the college. My Mom finally talked him into let me out.

Head Games for Prols and the Filthy Rich

Like the Lish-man we says
Yowsah, yowsah, yowsah
even as the papers just
flip up news bites

Two columns to feed the gonzo:
the lead, this week's wannabes
buy deep into scars   (à la stars)
strategically, surgically placed

Like on the chin means cut up
in bars, on the lip
cut up in love
                    the cheek
look out for a touch of old-
world chivalry, knight-errantry
Tongue's limp politesse

Next piece, predictable, ratchet
it up, goes for the throat
the Word RTF Frankenstein re-
write
        ** Full Head Transplant **
Doc Hollywood waxing frothy, the
"holy grail for neurosurgery"
(neuro-script on *giving* head?)

The downside?   Slice of quad city
below the neck, being frank, a bit stiff
Upside –   hey DH say cut above,
& heads off, "premature organ failure"

Not to forget "elderly or dying
millionaires"   Shake money maker
ports & folios looped on
late boomer reruns

Yowsah, yowsah, yessir
carvin' up the carcass
en masse, so to say, x-
treme make-over whose

alien, untouchable
desire. . .

Radio Clips Dad Missed from the 21st Century (Deflowered, out of the mouths of babes)

It's "hump nite" on Rock 99 &
winning tickets to the ball game
go to the 15-yr-old chicklet who
calls in the "complete-the-sentence"
contest
  The first time I had sex... dot dot dot
with that terminally bored
deadpan (past perfect)
of the perennial teen:
    I did it doggie style
in the little windmill house at the putt-putt
& banged my head getting up.

One can almost make out, peering
up ramp at the well flagged hole,
one of those ticky-boo pieces of Olde
Dutch real estate
    (windmill castle of yore
      clogs slipped off
        by outer stair

at the exact watershed moment our
late-blooming headbanger was taken
a-back, so to speak broadsided
by a decidedly enduring form
of lo-grade folk finesse.

Psych Nurse

Want you so bad
I can taste you
– like flakes of metal
Or those knock-out
pills you (seductive)
slip under my tongue
Wished instead my whole face
full of your lovely Polish
mouth

Spurned flatterer, might
I suggest you eat my
evidently unwanted number
(wouldn't presume ask
for yours)
           swallow it
with a gravol chaser,
let your gorgeous eyes
roll